I0813076

Lift High the Cross

FIVE SOLAS, FIVE PIANO ARRANGEMENTS

JENNY JEE-EL PARK

JUBAL HOUSE

EXCLUSIVELY DISTRIBUTED BY HAL•LEONARD® CORPORATION

BREHM CENTER

www.jubalhouse.com www.halleonard.com www.brehmcenter.com

Grace Greater than Our Sin
(Sola gratia)

MOODY: by Daniel B. Towner
Arr. by Jenny Jee-El Park

Cantabile ♩ = 64

8va
18
Grace,
grace,
God's
(8va)
21
grace,
1
grace that will
par - don and
24
cleanse with - in.
2
grace that is
8vb
27
great - er than
all our sin.
rit.
a tempo

31
Dark is the stain that we can - not hide. What can a -
f
8vb
36
vail to wash it a - way? Look! there is
8va
3
8vb
8vb
8vb
8vb
40
flow - ing a crim - son
6
9
42
tide;
6
6
6
6
6
6
(whole tone scale)
43
Both hands 8va
Whit - er than snow you may be to - day.

8va
(L.H. loco)
(8va)
(quasi-glissando)
5
2nd time to Coda
8va
5

63
8va
Mar - vel - ous, in - fi - nite, match - less grace
67
(8va)
free - ly be - stowed on all who be - lieve:
71
(8va)
You that are long - ing to see His face,
75
(8va)
will you this mo - ment His grace re - ceive?
8vb
79
(8va)

82
85
D.S. al Coda
8vb
8vb
CODA
88
8va
(8va)
92

When Jesus Wept
Lift High the Cross
(Solus Christus)

WHEN JESUS WEPT: by William Billings
CRUCIFER: by Sydney H. Nicholson
Arr. by Jenny Jee-El Park

*Lift High the Cross (George W. Kitchin, alt. Michael R. Newbolt / Sydney H. Nicholson)

Christ the Son of God.
rit. ed allargando
(8vb)
Triumphantly ♩ = 96
Lift high the cross, the love of Christ pro - claim, Till
ff
all the world a - dore His sa - cred name.
poco rit.
8va
Ethereal ♩ = 80
For Thy blest cross which doth for all a - tone, Cre -
pp
una corda
tre corde
8vb

a - tion's prais - es raise be - fore Thy throne.
43
poco a poco cresc.
8vb
47
8vb
rit.
(8vb)
Maestoso ♩ = 96
ff bring out melody
8vb
8vb
50
53
8vb
8vb
56
rit.
ff
8va
8vb

How Firm a Foundation
A Mighty Fortress Is Our God
(Sola scriptura)

FOUNDATION: Traditional American Melody
EIN' FESTE BURG: Martin Luther
Arr. by Jenny Jee-El Park

Allegro ma leggiero ♩ = 160

said, To you who for ref - uge to
Je - sus have fled?

Slower, with freedom
Tempo I
Slower, with freedom
8vb

Scherzando (playful) ♩= 182
That word a - bove all earth - ly pow'rs, no thanks to them a - bid - eth.
The Spir - it and the gifts are ours
2nd time to Coda
through Him who with us sid - eth.
Let
simile
mf

Chorale-like
59
goods and kin - dred go, this mor - tal life al -
65
so. The bod - y they may kill;
Slower, with freedom
70
God's truth
f
8vb
72
a - bid - eth still.
8vb
75
His king - dom is for - ev - er.
D.S. al Coda

Coda
78
rit. e dim.
81
pp
poco a poco cresc.
84
88
ff
3
8vb

If You Will Only Let God Guide You
Faith of Our Fathers
(Sola fide)

WER NUR DEN LIEBEN GOTT: by Georg Neumark
ST. CATHERINE: by Henri F. Hemy
Arr. by Jenny Jee-El Park

17
e - vil days. Who trusts in God's un -
21
chang - ing love Builds on a rock that
25
can - not move.
pp
Rubato ♩ = ca. 120
29
Faith of our fa - thers! liv - ing still in spite of dun - geon,
32
fire ___ and sword; Oh, how our hearts ___ beat high ___ with joy

when - e'er we hear that glo - rious word!
Faith of our fa - thers, ho - ly faith! We will be true to
Thee till death! Faith of our fa - thers, ho - ly faith!
We will be true to thee till death!
f
pp
una corda
ppp
8vb
8va
Cadenza (freely)
6
6

47
Tempo I
On - ly be still, and
tre corde
51
wait His lei - sure In cheer - ful hope, with
55
heart con - tent To take what - e'er the
59
Fa - ther's pleas - ure And all - dis - cern - ing
63
love have sent. Nor doubt our in - most

67
wants are known To Him who chose us
71
for His own. God hears the call of
75
those in need, The souls that trust in
79
Him in - deed.
rit.
8vb
83
Cadenza (freely)
8va
6
6

Let the whole creation cry: Alleluia!
"Glory to the Lord on high!" Alleluia!
Heaven and earth, awake and sing, Alleluia!
God is God and therefore King! Alleluia!

Let the Whole Creation Cry

(Soli Deo gloria)

LLANFAIR: by Robert Williams
Arr. by Jenny Jee-El Park

10
8va
8va
13
8va
(8va)
8va
15
(8va)
17
19
8va
8va
8vb

(8va)
8vb
8vb
8vb
8vb
(8vb)
8va
(8vb)
8va

31
(8va)
8va
mp
8vb
34
(8va)
8vb
8vb
36
6
6
6
8vb
38
8va
6
6
6
7
(8vb)
40
8va
6
6
8vb

41
Calando
p
rit.
Andante
mp
44
46
3
49
rit.
8va
51
p
cresc.

53
8va
8vb
55
5
5
6
6
allargando e pesante
(8vb)
8vb
8vb
58
(8vb)
8vb
8va
61
8vb
8vb
8va
64
(8va)
8va

67
8va
8vb
70
8va
ff
(8vb)
72
(8va)
74
(8va)
mf
76
sub. p
poco a poco cresc.

78
gliss.
rit.
8va
80
82
6
6
83
86

SOLA FIDE · SOLI DEO GLORIA · SOLA SCRIPTURA · SOLUS CHRISTUS · SOLA GRATIA

semper reformanda

THE FIVE SOLAS PROJECT

Resources in the Five Solas Music project are:

Five songs for children's choir based on the five sola themes:

- **WE BELIEVE (CREED)** – Faith Alone
- **DEEP, DEEP LOVE OF JESUS** – Christ Alone
- **GRACE, GOD'S GRACE** – Grace Alone
- **O WORD OF GOD (SO STRONG AND TRUE)** – Scripture Alone
- **GLORY BE TO GOD** – Glory to God Alone

Listening CD, stereo and split tracks, and chord charts are available.

There is a Five Solas Resource Pak for directors/teachers. The resource pak includes stories, responsive readings, devotional guides with discussion questions, and copyable activities to enhance the experience of focusing on each of the five sola themes.

Also for children and teachers/parents is a fully illustrated storybook, **GROWING GOD'S WAY**. The five stories invite an imaginative look at each of the sola themes. A music CD is included to further enhance the storytelling experience.

LIFT HIGH THE CROSS and **JESUS LOVES ME** are collections of piano and organ solos, respectively, that focus attention on the sola themes. These artistic offerings are intended to challenge pianists and organists musically, while at the same time providing creative keyboard resources for worship.